- Some claim that Islamic law is restrictive of essential liberties and incompatible with advanced civilizations and modern concepts of human rights. In fact, this widely propagated misconception has been addressed many times in numerous books and forums worldwide.

- We note here that Muslims believe Islamic law is a complete and comprehensive code of life, fully adaptable and suitable in its principles and laws for every age, location, and people.

DID YOU KNOW?

- True liberty is freedom from subservience to oppression, whether it comes from one's own selfish desires or from a ruling oligarchy. The worst form of subservience is to worship others besides the One Lord, Creator, and Sustainer of humankind. Islam does not accept the so-called liberty of the libertine who believes he may do whatever he desires, including committing crimes.

Did You Know?

DID YOU KNOW?

- Islam is not only a religion of the spiritual bond between a person and his Lord and Creator, but it also includes temporal and worldly commandments from God, the Wise, governing all aspects of life. Islam organizes the relationship between human beings and their Creator, as well as relationships within society and with other nations. Unlike Judaism, Islam is universal and is not limited to a specific nation or people. Although Christians claim universality, they have, according to Islamic belief, diverged from the path revealed to Jesus, who said, as recorded in the Bible: "I was sent only to the lost sheep of the house of Israel."

Did You Know?

- Jesus is also reported to have said to his twelve disciples, who were chosen to correspond to the twelve tribes of Israel: "These twelve Jesus sent out and commanded them, saying, 'Do not go among the Gentiles or enter any town of the Samaritans. Go rather to the lost sheep of the house of Israel.'"

- The Prophet of Islam was sent as a mercy to all humankind. God, the Exalted, states in the Qur'an: "We have sent you only as a mercy to the worlds.". (21:107)

- The Islamic Shari'ah has two aspects. One aspect includes matters of faith, belief, various acts of worship, and laws that are constant and not subject to change, regardless of differences in time or place. For instance, prayer in Islam is a ritual with standard specifications, whether in the UK, the US, Nigeria, Arabia, or Malaysia. Similarly, Zakah (obligatory charity) has standardized and unalterable rates and amounts for various categories of wealth. The laws of inheritance are fixed, and no one in society has the right to modify them for any reason.

- These permanent laws reinforce the underlying equality among all people, since they are essentially the same wherever they live.

DID YOU KNOW?

- The second aspect of the Islamic Shari'ah consists of laws—especially those that regulate relationships between people and with other nations—which are presented in a general form, with the details left to be adapted according to the needs that arise in constantly changing social conditions. Such rules and regulations may be amended, altered, and adapted within this general framework. These changes or modifications, however, must be supervised by specialists and jurists who thoroughly understand the principles of Islamic law and the developments of contemporary society. The principle of consultation (Shura) is one example.

- This principle is mentioned in the Qur'an in a general form, without detailing its mechanics. The Qur'an does not provide binding instructions on exactly how to apply, execute, or implement Shura in Islamic society, although the Sunnah (Way) of the Prophet offers some guidance. This adaptability allows Islamic scholars to interpret the details of Shura to meet the requirements of every age and place.

DID YOU KNOW?

- What is applicable to one generation or society can be made applicable to another with minor adjustments according to the needs of the time. This flexibility demonstrates the validity, comprehensiveness, and universal scope of Islam.

Misconception #2

DID YOU KNOW?

- Some who are unaware of the basic truths about Islam—whether pseudo-scholars, Orientalists, or opponents of Islam—claim that Islam does not respect the legal rights of non-Muslims in an Islamic state. The Islamic Shari'ah provides a distinct set of obligations and rights for non-Muslim residents within Islamic society.

- It may be sufficient, in rebuttal of this misconception, to quote the general ruling mentioned in the books of Islamic jurisprudence: "Non-Muslims are entitled to that which Muslims are entitled, and they are obligated to do that which Muslims are obligated to do."

DID YOU KNOW?

- This is the general rule, and from it emanate just and equitable laws granting non-Muslim residents in an Islamic state their rights to security, private property, religious observance, and other protections. Islam permits religious discussions and dialogue with non-Muslims, commanding Muslims to adhere to the best methods in their interactions with them.

- God, the Exalted and Majestic, states in the Qur'an: "And do not argue with the People of the Scripture except in a manner that is best, except with those who commit injustice among them, and say, 'We believe in that which has been revealed to us and revealed to you. Our God and your God is One, and to Him we submit.'" (29:46)

Did You Know?

- God addresses those of other faiths and religions in the Qur'an: "Say, [O Muhammad], 'Have you considered that which you invoke besides Allah? Show me what they have created of the earth, or whether they have any partnership in the heavens. Bring me a scripture revealed before this or a trace of knowledge, if you are truthful.'" (46:4)

- Islam forbids the use of force to convert people of other faiths, as stated in the Qur'an: "If it had been your Lord's will, all who are on earth would have believed. Will you then compel mankind, against their will, to believe?" (10:99)

Did You Know?

- Both the Qur'an and the Sunnah (traditions of the Prophet) demonstrate that freedom of religion is granted to members of society under Islamic Shari'ah. Muslim history provides numerous examples of tolerance shown to non-Muslim communities, while many other societies were intolerant toward Muslims and even toward their own people.

- Muslims must deal justly with all people who have not initiated hostilities against them. God states in the Qur'an: "God does not forbid you, with regard to those who do not fight you because of your faith nor drive you out of your homes, from dealing kindly and justly with them. Indeed, God loves those who are just." (60:8)

Did You Know?

- Those who wage war against Islam, show enmity, and force Muslims into exile are treated differently under Islamic law. God, the Exalted, states in the Glorious Qur'an: "It is only regarding those who fight you because of religion, and who drive you out of your homes or assist in driving you out, that God forbids you from befriending them. Whoever befriends them — then such are the wrongdoers." (60:9)

DID YOU KNOW?

- Interactions between Muslims and non-Muslims are based on cordial and just conduct. Commercial transactions are permitted with both resident and non-resident non-Muslims within Islamic society. A Muslim may eat the food of Jews and Christians. A Muslim man may marry a Jewish or Christian woman, as will be explained below. We must remember that Islam places special attention and importance on raising a family.

- God, the Sublime, states in the Qur'an: "This day all things good and pure are made lawful for you. The food of the People of the Book is lawful for you, and your food is lawful for them. Lawful for you in marriage are not only chaste women who are Believers, but also chaste women among the People of the Book, revealed before your time, provided you give them their due dowry and desire chastity, not lewdness or secret intrigues. If anyone rejects faith, their work is fruitless, and in the Hereafter they will be among the losers." (5:5)

DID YOU KNOW?

Misconception #3

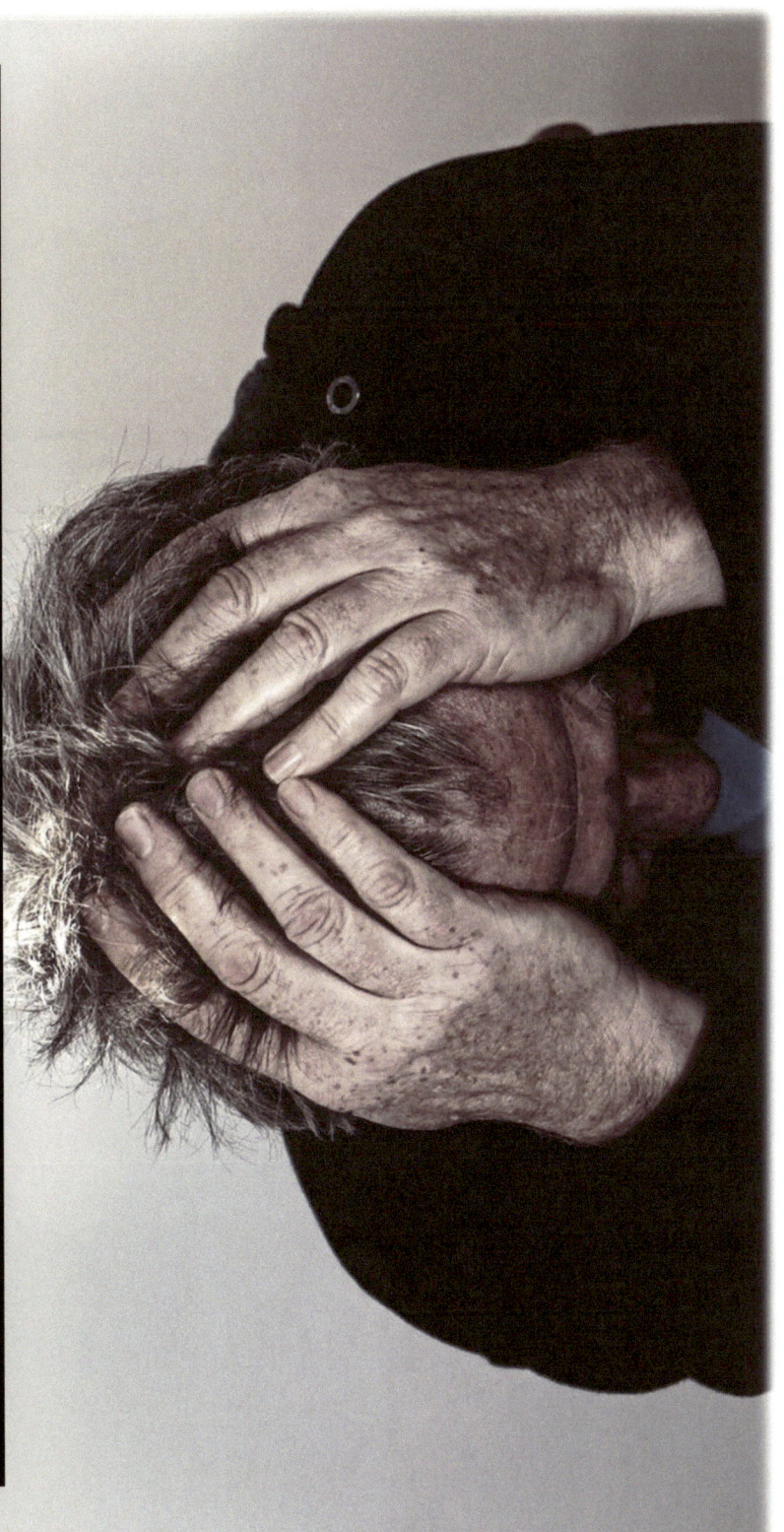

DID YOU KNOW?

- Many claim that the punishment prescribed in Islam for apostasy is a violation of human rights. The modern concept of human rights guarantees freedom of religion for all people. They argue that this punishment contradicts what God, the Exalted and Almighty, states in the Glorious Qur'an: "Let there be no compulsion in religion." (2:256)

DID YOU KNOW?

- The well-known tradition of the Prophet states: "The blood of a Muslim may not be lawfully shed except in one of three cases: a married person who commits adultery; a life for a life; and one who abandons his religion (Islam) and separates himself from the community."

- The Prophet also said: "Whoever changes his religion (Islam), execute him."

- Without a doubt, this is a highly contentious issue within the Muslim community and a matter of disagreement among scholars. The reasons for this disagreement are as follows:

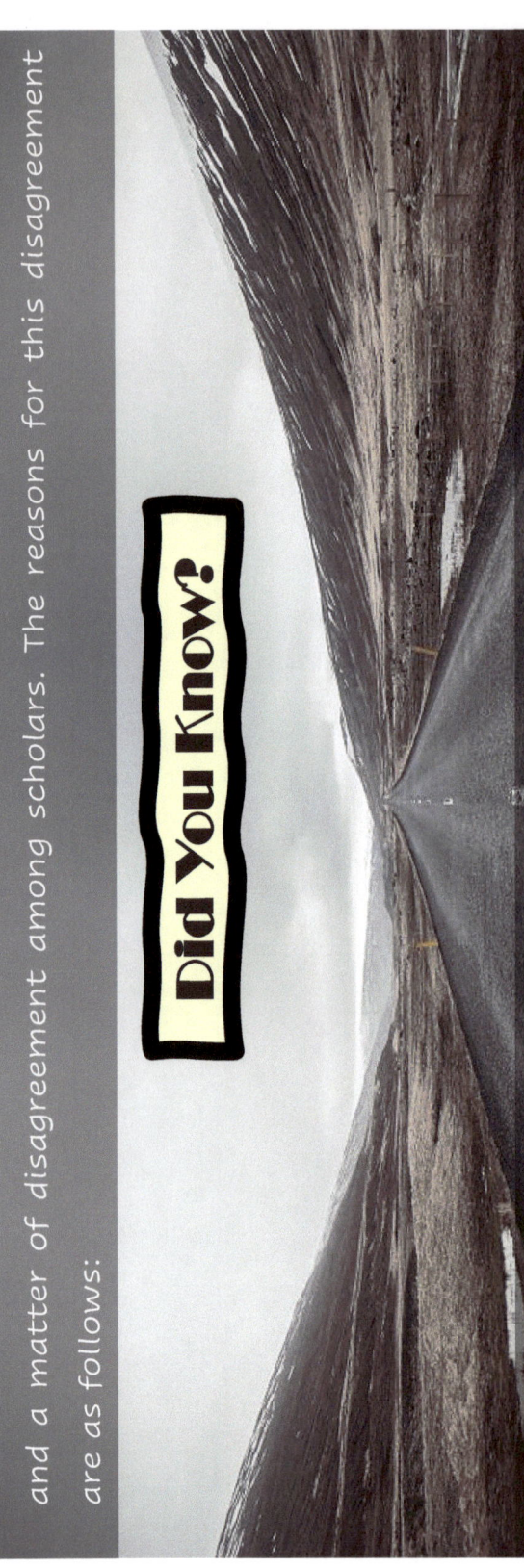

Did You Know?

1. There is no capital punishment for apostasy mentioned in the Qur'an.
2. The aforementioned hadith provide only part of the picture and are not definitive in their meanings.
3. The Prophet Muhammad is our example in Islam, yet there is clear evidence of people leaving Islam during his lifetime, and he did not order their execution. Therefore, there appears to be missing historical context.

DID YOU KNOW?

- If we look more deeply into the hadith, we find an equally authentic report that clarifies the hadith mentioned above. 'Aisha, the Prophet's wife, narrated that the Messenger of God said: "The blood of a Muslim who testifies that none has the right to be worshipped but Allah and that I am His Messenger cannot be shed except in three cases: a married person who commits adultery — he is to be stoned; a person who goes out fighting against God and His Messenger — he is to be killed, crucified, or exiled from the land; and a person who murders another — he is to be killed in retaliation."

- This authentic version of the Prophet's statement sheds more light on the issue. Specifically, it clarifies that it is not the act of apostasy alone that mandates capital punishment, but rather the typical consequence of apostasy — fighting against the community of believers in conjunction with the apostasy — that leads to such punishment.

Did You Know?

DID YOU KNOW?

- Thus, we can understand the Islamic verdict regarding apostasy as follows:
1. If a person abandons the religion and leaves the community without fighting or attacking it, then they are left to live their lives, and no harm comes to them. This is how the Prophet handled such cases, as seen in his history (Seerah).

DID YOU KNOW?

2. If a person abandons the religion and then joins the enemies of the community to fight against it, the Islamic government has the option to execute or imprison the individual, depending on what it deems appropriate. This is consistent with the hadith of 'Aisha mentioned above.

3. If a person abandons the religion but does not leave the community or fight against it, then his case is referred to the scholars and counselors of the Islamic government. They will assess why he made this decision and whether he may have been deceived or is not of sound mind. If he is found to be sane, fully aware of his decision, and persists in his apostasy, then he is exiled.

DID YOU KNOW?

- It is important to note that, regardless of the situation, the issue of execution is an executive decision to be made solely by the government and is never to be taken into the hands of the public. If such a person confines his disbelief and apostasy to himself and does not proclaim or propagate it, he is left to God and the punishments of the Hereafter.

- God knows best who believes and who rejects faith, who is sincere, and who is a hypocrite. Muslim authorities base their judgments and rulings only on outward, observable matters and leave the inner realities to God.

A

- Allah: The name Muslims use for God, who made everything.
- Akhlaq: Being kind, polite, and good to everyone.
- Ablution (Wudu): Washing hands, face, and feet before praying.
- Adhan: A call to prayer to tell everyone it's time to pray.
- Alhamdulillah: Saying "Thank you, Allah!" for all the blessings He gives us.
- Al-Quran: The holy book of Islam, which teaches us how to live a good life.
- Amal: Doing good actions that make Allah happy.
- Ameen: A word we say at the end of a dua, meaning "Please accept it, Allah!"
- Angels (Malaikah): Special beings made by Allah to do His work, like bringing messages or protecting us.
- Arafah: A special day during Hajj when pilgrims pray on a big plain.
- Ar-Rahman: One of Allah's names, meaning "The Most Merciful."
- Ar-Raheem: Another name of Allah, meaning "The Most Kind."
- Ashura: A special day in the Islamic calendar when we remember important events.

- Ayah: A verse in the Quran that teaches us something about Allah and life.
- Aqidah: Believing in Allah and His teachings as the foundation of our faith.

B

- Bismillah: It means "In the name of Allah," said before starting anything good.
- Barakah: Special blessings and goodness from Allah.
- Burqa: A piece of clothing some Muslim women wear to cover themselves.
- Bab-ul-Rahmah: The Gate of Mercy in a mosque, like a special door.
- Bilal: A companion of Prophet Muhammad (peace be upon him) and the first person to call the Adhan.
- Badr: The name of an important battle where Muslims prayed to Allah for help and won with His support.
- Baitullah: Another name for the Kaaba, meaning "The House of Allah."

- Bukhari: A famous collection of Hadith (sayings of Prophet Muhammad, peace be upon him).
- Baraqah (Buraq): A special creature that carried Prophet Muhammad (peace be upon him) on his night journey to the heavens.
- Bay'ah: A promise made by people to follow and obey their leader in Islam.
- Birr: Being good and kind, especially to your parents.
- Burhan: Clear evidence or proof, like the Quran, that shows Allah's truth.
- Baqi: A famous graveyard in Madinah where many of the Prophet's companions are buried.
- Bismillah-ir-Rahman-ir-Raheem: The full phrase meaning "In the name of Allah, the Most Merciful, the Most Kind," often said at the start of the Quran's chapters.
- Bayan: A speech or talk given to explain Islamic teachings and inspire people.

C

- Caliph: A leader who helps guide the Muslim community.
- Charity (Sadaqah): Giving to people in need to make them happy.
- Camel: An animal important in Islamic history, often used in desert journeys.
- Companions (Sahabah): Friends of Prophet Muhammad (peace be upon him).

Here's an expanded list of 11 more terminologies under C with simple explanations suitable for children:

- Cave of Hira: The special place where Prophet Muhammad (peace be upon him) first received Allah's message.
- Creation: Everything Allah made, like people, animals, trees, and stars.
- Crescent: A curved moon shape that is often seen on mosques and used to start Islamic months.
- Commandments: Important rules from Allah that teach us how to live a good life.
- Community (Ummah): All Muslims around the world who follow Islam.
- Clarity: The feeling of understanding when Allah helps us know what's right.
- Comfort: The peace we feel when we trust Allah to take care of us.

- Compassion: Caring for others just like Allah cares for us.
- Cleanliness: Staying clean and pure, which is very important in Islam.
- Converts: People who choose to follow Islam later in their lives.
- Celebration: Happy times like Eid when Muslims come together to pray, eat, and share joy.

D

- Dua: Talking to Allah and asking for help or saying thank you.
- Deen: A word that means religion or way of life in Islam.
- Dawood (David): A prophet who loved to sing and praised Allah.
- Dhikr: Remembering Allah by saying words like "SubhanAllah" (Glory to Allah).
- Dua: Talking to Allah and asking for help or saying thank you.
- Deen: A word that means religion or way of life in Islam.
- Dawood (David): A prophet who loved to sing and praised Allah.
- Dhikr: Remembering Allah by saying words like "SubhanAllah" (Glory to Allah).
- Darul Aman: A place of peace and safety.
- Dawah: Inviting others to learn about and understand Islam.

- Dajjal: A deceiver mentioned in Islamic eschatology who will appear before the Day of Judgment.
- Darul Harb: Lands not governed by Islamic law, often referred to as territories of conflict.
- Darul Islam: Lands governed by Islamic law, promoting peace and justice.
- Dirham: A silver coin used as currency in early Islamic history.
- Dhul-Hijjah: The twelfth and final month of the Islamic lunar calendar, in which Hajj takes place.
- Dhul-Qarnayn: A figure mentioned in the Quran known for his just rule and building barriers to protect people from harm.
- Dunya: Refers to this world and its temporary nature compared to the eternal Hereafter.

E

- Eid: A happy celebration after Ramadan or Hajj, with prayers, sweets, and gifts.
- Eman (Iman): Believing in Allah and His teachings with your heart.
- Ehsan: Being extra kind and doing your best in everything.
- Eidgah: A big open place where Muslims pray together on Eid.
- Eid: A happy celebration after Ramadan or Hajj, with prayers, sweets, and gifts.
- Eman (Iman): Believing in Allah and His teachings with your heart.
- Ehsan: Being extra kind and doing your best in everything.
- Eidgah: A big open place where Muslims pray together on Eid.
- Eid ul-Fitr: The festival marking the end of Ramadan, celebrated with joy and charity.

- Eid ul-Adha: The festival of sacrifice, remembering Prophet Ibrahim's obedience to Allah.
- Ebadah (Ibadah): Acts of worship like praying, fasting, and being good to others.
- Eblis: Another name for Shaytan (Satan), who disobeyed Allah.
- Eeman (Faith): A strong belief in Allah, His angels, books, prophets, the Day of Judgment, and destiny.
- Ehtikaf (Itikaf): Staying in the mosque for worship, especially during the last ten days of Ramadan.
- Ehsanul Khaliqeen: A name of Allah meaning "The Best of Creators."
- Eid Mubarak: A greeting exchanged during Eid, meaning "Blessed Eid."
- Eid Salat: The special prayer offered on the morning of Eid.

F

- Fajr: The first prayer of the day, done at dawn.
- Fasting (Sawm): Not eating or drinking from dawn to sunset in Ramadan.
- Fard: Something Allah tells us we must do, like praying five times a day.
- Fiqh: Rules that help us understand what is right and wrong in Islam.
- Fatiha: The first chapter of the Quran, recited in every unit of prayer.
- Faith (Iman): Believing in Allah, His angels, His books, His messengers, the Last Day, and destiny.
- Fitnah: A trial or test that challenges faith or causes trouble.
- Fidyah: Compensation given for missing a fast, such as feeding the poor.
- Fitrah: The natural disposition or state humans are born with, inclined toward worshiping Allah.
- Fard Kifayah: A communal obligation, like attending a funeral prayer, where some members of the community fulfill it on behalf of others.
- Furqan: Another name for the Quran, meaning "the criterion" that distinguishes right from wrong.
- Fajr Sunnah: The two recommended units of prayer before the obligatory Fajr prayer.

- Fiqh-ul-Ibadat: The study of rules related to worship, such as prayer, fasting, and pilgrimage.
- Farah: A state of joy and happiness that pleases Allah.
- Fuqaha: Scholars who are experts in Islamic jurisprudence (Fiqh).

G

- Gabriel (Jibreel): An angel who brought Allah's messages to prophets.
- Ghusl: A special bath to clean yourself before praying or after certain events.
- Grateful (Shukr): Saying thank you to Allah for everything He gives us.
- Guidance: Help from Allah to do what is right and stay on the good path.
- Gabriel (Jibreel): An angel who brought Allah's messages to prophets.
- Ghusl: A special bath to clean yourself before praying or after certain events.
- Grateful (Shukr): Saying thank you to Allah for everything He gives us.
- Guidance: Help from Allah to do what is right and stay on the good path.
- Ghafir: One of Allah's names, meaning "The Forgiving."
- Ghadab: The word for anger in Arabic, which believers are encouraged to control.

- Garden (Jannah): The beautiful place of paradise Allah promises to the good.
- Good Deeds (A'mal Salih): Actions that please Allah, like helping others and being kind.
- Generosity: Sharing what you have with others for the sake of Allah.
- Ghaib: Things that are unseen, like angels and the Day of Judgment, which we believe in through faith.
- Golden Rule: Treating others the way you want to be treated, as taught in Islam.
- Grave (Qabr): The place where a person is buried and where the journey to the Hereafter begins.
- Ghaffar: Another name of Allah, meaning "The Oft-Forgiving."

H

- Hajj: A special trip to the Kaaba in Makkah that Muslims make once in their life if they can.
- Halal: Things that are allowed for Muslims, like certain foods.
- Haram: Things that are not allowed in Islam, like lying or stealing.
- Hijab: A scarf some Muslim women wear to cover their hair.
- Hijrah: The journey Prophet Muhammad (peace be upon him) took from Makkah to Madinah.
- Hadith: The sayings and actions of Prophet Muhammad (peace be upon him) that teach Muslims how to live.
- Hafiz: A person who has memorized the entire Quran.
- Halq: The shaving of the head, often done after completing Hajj or Umrah.
- Hamzah: One of Prophet Muhammad's (peace be upon him) uncles who was known for his bravery and became a martyr.
- Haneef: Someone who follows the pure monotheistic way of worshipping Allah.
- Haram (Sanctuary): A sacred area, like the Masjid al-Haram in Makkah or Masjid an-Nabawi in Madinah.
- Hasanat: Good deeds that earn rewards from Allah.

- Hudhud: The hoopoe bird mentioned in the Quran in the story of Prophet Sulaiman (Solomon).
- Hudood: The limits set by Allah, such as laws for society and worship.
- Hikmah: Wisdom or understanding given by Allah.
- Houri: Beautiful beings mentioned in the Quran as a reward in Paradise.

I

- Islam: The religion of peace and submission to Allah.
- Ihsan: Doing good deeds in the best way possible, with love for Allah.
- Iftar: The meal Muslims eat to break their fast in Ramadan.
- Imam: A leader who guides the prayer in a mosque.
- InshaAllah: It means "If Allah wills," said when planning something.
- Ibadah: Acts of worship performed to please Allah, such as prayer and fasting.
- Ilm: Knowledge or the pursuit of learning, highly valued in Islam.
- Ikhlas: Sincerity and purity of intention in worship and actions.
- Israa: The miraculous night journey of Prophet Muhammad (PBUH) from Mecca to Jerusalem.

- Iblis: The name of Satan, who disobeyed Allah and was cast out of Heaven.
- Ijma: Consensus or agreement among Islamic scholars on religious matters.
- Ihsan: Excellence in worship and character, striving for perfection in actions.
- Iqra: The first word revealed to Prophet Muhammad (PBUH), meaning "Read."
- Iddah: The waiting period a woman observes after divorce or the death of her husband.
- Ismail (Ishmael): A prophet, the son of Ibrahim (Abraham), known for his patience and obedience.
- Imaan: Faith or belief in Allah, His prophets, and His teachings.

J

- Jannah: Paradise, the beautiful garden where good people go after they die.
- Jinn: Invisible beings created by Allah from smokeless fire.
- Jumu'ah: The special prayer on Friday for Muslims.
- Justice (Adl): Being fair and treating everyone kindly.
- Jibreel (Gabriel): The angel who brought Allah's messages to the prophets.
- Jahannam: Hell, a place for those who do not follow Allah's guidance.
- Jam'ah: A group prayer performed together.
- Janazah: The Islamic funeral prayer for the deceased.

- Juz: One of the 30 parts of the Quran for easier reading and memorization.
- Jaiz: Something allowed or permissible in Islam.
- Jihad: Striving or struggling for a good cause, especially to live according to Allah's guidance.
- Jilbab: A long, loose-fitting coat or outer garment worn by some Muslim women.
- Jadid: A term meaning "new" or "fresh" in Arabic.
- Jamrah: A pillar representing Satan that Muslims throw stones at during Hajj.
- Jabbar: One of Allah's names, meaning "The Compeller" or "The All-Powerful."

K

- Kaaba: The black cube in Makkah that Muslims pray towards.
- Khalifa: A person chosen to take care of Allah's creations and lead with goodness.
- Kindness: Being nice and caring for people, animals, and nature.
- Kiswa: The black cloth that covers the Kaaba.
- Kaaba: The black cube in Makkah that Muslims pray towards.
- Khalifa: A person chosen to take care of Allah's creations and lead with goodness.
- Kindness: Being nice and caring for people, animals, and nature.
- Kiswa: The black cloth that covers the Kaaba.
- Kalima: A declaration of faith in Islam, meaning "There is no god but Allah, and Muhammad is His Messenger."
- Khutbah: A sermon or speech, especially the one given during the Friday prayer (Jumu'ah).

- Kaba'il: Tribes or groups of people in Arab culture.
- Khair: Goodness or blessings.
- Kufr: Denial or disbelief in Allah.
- Kanz: Treasure or something precious.
- Kitab: Book, often referring to the holy books revealed by Allah.
- Karim: Generous or noble, one of Allah's attributes (Al-Karim).
- Khalil: Close friend, often used to refer to Prophet Ibrahim as "Khalilullah" (Friend of Allah).

L

- Lailatul Qadr: A special night in Ramadan when prayers are extra powerful.
- Love: Caring deeply for Allah, family, friends, and all His creations.
- Luqman: A wise man mentioned in the Quran who gave good advice to his son.
- Learning (Ilm): Gaining knowledge to understand the world and become closer to Allah.
- Lailatul Qadr: A special night in Ramadan when prayers are extra powerful.
- Love: Caring deeply for Allah, family, friends, and all His creations.
- Luqman: A wise man mentioned in the Quran who gave good advice to his son.
- Learning (Ilm): Gaining knowledge to understand the world and become closer to Allah.

- Lutf (Kindness): Allah's gentle care and mercy toward His creations.
- Lisan (Tongue): The part of the body used for speaking, which should always say good words.
- Labbayk: A word meaning "I am here," often said during Hajj to respond to Allah's call.
- Lillah: Something done purely for the sake of Allah.
- Lantern (Fanous): A traditional decorative light, often used during Ramadan.
- Loyalty: Being faithful and committed to Allah and His teachings.
- Layyin (Softness): Being gentle and soft in speech and behavior, as taught in Islam.
- Light (Noor): A symbol of guidance and purity, often associated with Allah's guidance.
- Lament: Feeling regret or sorrow, turning to Allah for forgiveness.

M

- Makkah: The holiest city for Muslims where the Kaaba is located.
- Masjid: Another word for mosque, a place where Muslims pray.
- Mercy (Rahma): Allah's kindness and forgiveness for everyone.
- Madinah: The city where Prophet Muhammad (peace be upon him) is buried.
- Minaret: The tall tower of a mosque from where the call to prayer is made.
- Mihrab: A niche in the wall of a mosque that indicates the direction of the Kaaba in Makkah (Qibla), toward which Muslims pray.
- Minbar: A pulpit in the mosque where the imam delivers the Friday sermon (Khutbah).
- Muezzin: The person who calls Muslims to prayer from the minaret of a mosque.

- Mahr: A mandatory gift or dowry given by the groom to the bride in Islamic marriage.
- Mufti: An Islamic scholar qualified to issue legal opinions or fatwas.
- Mujahid: A person engaged in jihad, striving or struggling in the way of Allah.
- Mahram: A close relative with whom marriage is forbidden, providing a lawful level of interaction.
- Mukallaf: A person who is legally responsible in Islamic law, having reached maturity and sanity.
- Mubah: Actions in Islam that are permissible and neither rewarded nor punished.
- Mushaf: A physical copy of the Qur'an.
- Masjid al-Haram: The Sacred Mosque in Makkah, encompassing the Kaaba and the holiest site in Islam.

N

- Nabi: A prophet chosen by Allah to guide people.
- Nafs: Our inner self that sometimes needs to be taught patience.
- Nikah: A marriage ceremony in Islam.

- Noor: Light, often used to describe Allah's guidance or blessings.
- Nasihah: Sincere advice or guidance given for the benefit of others.
- Niyyah: Intention, a key aspect in Islam as actions are judged by their intentions.
- Nasr: Help or victory granted by Allah.
- Nabi-ul-Ummi: A title of Prophet Muhammad (peace be upon him), meaning "The Unlettered Prophet."
- Nafs-e-Mutmainnah: The contented soul, one at peace with Allah's will.
- Nifaq: Hypocrisy, considered a severe spiritual ailment in Islam.
- Nawafil: Voluntary prayers or acts of worship beyond the obligatory ones.

- Nahr: Ritual animal sacrifice performed during Eid-ul-Adha.
- Nur-ul-Quran: The light and guidance derived from the Quran.
- Nuzul: The descent or revelation of the Quran upon the Prophet Muhammad (peace be upon him).
- Nasab: Lineage or ancestry, often emphasized in Islamic family and inheritance laws.

O

- Obedience: Listening to Allah and following His commands with love.
- Omar (Umar): A wise and strong companion of the Prophet Muhammad (peace be upon him).
- Offering (Sadaqah): Giving money or help to people in need to make them happy.
- Ottoman: A Muslim empire that ruled many lands long ago.
- Obligation (Fard): A required act in Islam that must be performed by every Muslim.
- Oneness (Tawheed): The belief in the unity and singularity of Allah, central to Islamic faith.
- Oasis: A fertile spot in the desert, often mentioned in Islamic history and geography.
- Orphans (Yatama): Children without parents, who hold a special place in Islam and are to be treated with care and compassion.
- Omar ibn Abdul Aziz: A revered Umayyad caliph known for his justice and piety.

- Oaths (Ayman): Swearing by Allah in serious matters, with emphasis on truthfulness.
- Oppression (Zulm): Any form of injustice or wrongdoing, strongly condemned in Islam.
- Oblation (Qurbani): The act of sacrificing an animal during Eid al-Adha to honor Prophet Ibrahim's devotion.
- Obedient Angels: Angels who fulfill Allah's commands without question or disobedience.
- Ordeal (Ibtilaa): A test or trial given by Allah to strengthen faith and patience.
- Olive (Zaytoon): A blessed fruit mentioned in the Qur'an, symbolizing purity and goodness.

P

- Prophet: A person Allah chose to teach people the right way, like Prophet Muhammad (peace be upon him).
- Patience (Sabr): Staying calm and trusting Allah during hard times.
- Prayer (Salah): Talking to Allah five times a day.
- Peace (Salaam): Being calm and kind to everyone around you.
- Paradise (Jannah): The eternal home of happiness and reward for those who follow Allah's guidance.
- Piety (Taqwa): Being mindful of Allah in all actions and decisions.
- Prostration (Sujood): Bowing down in humility and worship during Salah.

- Prophethood (Nubuwwah): The responsibility given by Allah to chosen individuals to guide humanity.

- Purity (Tahara): Staying clean in body, mind, and soul as part of faith.
- Pilgrimage (Hajj): A journey to Makkah required once in a lifetime for those who are able.
- Poverty (Faqr): A state that is not a punishment but a test and opportunity for gratitude and patience.
- People of the Book (Ahlul Kitab): Refers to Jews and Christians who received earlier scriptures.
- Punishment (Azaab): The consequence of disobedience to Allah, in this life or the Hereafter.
- Prophetic Traditions (Hadith): The sayings, actions, and approvals of Prophet Muhammad (peace be upon him).
- Promise (Wa'd): A commitment that must be fulfilled, reflecting honesty and trustworthiness.

Q

- Quran: The holy book of Islam, full of Allah's words.

- Qibla: The direction Muslims face when they pray, towards the Kaaba.
- Qadr (Destiny): Knowing that Allah has a plan for everything.
- Qunut: A special prayer said during some salahs.
- Quraysh: The prominent tribe of Makkah to which Prophet Muhammad (PBUH) belonged.
- Qisas: The principle of retributive justice in Islamic law.
- Qurban: The act of sacrificing an animal for Allah, especially during Eid al-Adha.
- Qalam: The "pen" used metaphorically in the Quran, representing knowledge and wisdom.
- Qari: A person who recites the Quran with proper tajweed and melodious tone.

- Qudsi Hadith: Sacred narrations where Allah's words are conveyed through the Prophet (PBUH), but not part of the Quran.
- Qayamat (Day of Judgment): The day when all souls will be resurrected for accountability.
- Qawwam: A term referring to the role of men as maintainers or protectors of women in the family.
- Qanun: Laws or regulations derived from Islamic principles.
- Qabr: The grave where a person is buried after death.
- Qalb: The heart, often referred to in Islamic teachings as the spiritual center of a person.

R

- Ramadan: The holy month when Muslims fast and do good deeds.
- Rahman: A name of Allah meaning "The Most Merciful."
- Respect: Treating everyone nicely because Allah loves kind people.
- Ruqyah: Prayers said to ask Allah for healing and protection.
- Rabi' al-Awwal: The third month in the Islamic calendar, known for the birth of Prophet Muhammad (PBUH).
- Raheem: A name of Allah meaning "The Most Compassionate."
- Raka'ah: A unit of prayer in Salah (Islamic prayer).
- Rajab: The seventh month in the Islamic calendar, considered one of the sacred months.
- Rizq: Sustenance or provision provided by Allah.

- Righteousness: Acting in a way that pleases Allah and aligns with His commands.
- Rahmah: Mercy or compassion, a key characteristic encouraged in Islam.
- Rumi: A famous Islamic poet and scholar known for his spiritual writings.
- Ruh: The soul or spirit, considered the essence of life.
- Ramadan Kareem: A common greeting during Ramadan meaning "Generous Ramadan."
- Rowdah: The sacred area in the Prophet's Mosque in Medina, often referred to as a garden of Paradise.

S

- Salah: The five daily prayers that Muslims do.
- Sawm: Fasting during Ramadan, where Muslims don't eat or drink from dawn to sunset.
- Shahada: The statement of belief: "There is no god but Allah, and Muhammad is His messenger."
- Shukr: Being thankful to Allah for all the blessings He gives.
- Sadaqah: Voluntary charity given to help others and earn Allah's pleasure.
- Sajdah: The act of prostration during prayer, showing humility before Allah.

- Sharia: The divine law derived from the Quran and Sunnah, guiding all aspects of a Muslim's life.
- Shirk: Associating partners with Allah, considered the gravest sin in Islam.

- SubhanAllah: An expression meaning "Glory be to Allah," used to praise His perfection.
- Sunnah: The teachings, actions, and sayings of Prophet Muhammad (PBUH).
- Surah: A chapter of the Quran; there are 114 Surahs in the Quran.
- Sidq: Truthfulness and honesty in words and actions.
- Sirat al-Mustaqeem: The Straight Path; the way of living that pleases Allah.
- Sabr: Patience and perseverance in the face of difficulties.
- Salam: Peace; often used as a greeting in the phrase "As-salamu alaykum" meaning "Peace be upon you."

T

- Taqwa: Being aware of Allah and trying to do what He loves.
- Tawheed: Believing in only one God, Allah.
- Tahajjud: A special prayer done at night, when everyone else is asleep.
- Tasbeeh: Saying words of praise like "SubhanAllah" (Glory to Allah) many times.
- Tafseer: The explanation or interpretation of the Quran.
- Taharah: The state of cleanliness or purity in Islam, often achieved through wudu (ablution) or ghusl (ritual bath).
- Takaful: Islamic mutual insurance based on shared responsibility and cooperation.
- Taqdeer: The concept of divine destiny or predestination in Islam.
- Tawaaf: The act of circling the Kaaba during Hajj or Umrah as a form of worship.

- Tawakkul: Placing complete trust and reliance on Allah while taking appropriate actions.
- Takbeer: The declaration "Allahu Akbar" (Allah is the Greatest), often said in prayers and other acts of worship.
- Tarawih: Special prayers performed in congregation during the nights of Ramadan.
- Tahneek: A Sunnah practice of softening a date and rubbing it on a newborn's palate.
- Talbiyah: A supplication made by pilgrims during Hajj or Umrah, beginning with "Labbayk Allahumma Labbayk."
- Tafakkur: Reflecting and pondering on the signs of Allah in the universe and creation.

U

- Umrah: A smaller pilgrimage to Makkah that Muslims can do anytime.
- Umar: A strong and wise companion of Prophet Muhammad (peace be upon him).
- Unity: Muslims coming together to help and care for each other.
- Udhiyah: Sacrificing an animal like a sheep during Eid-ul-Adha to remember Prophet Ibrahim's (Abraham's) story.
- Usrah: A small group gathering of Muslims for learning and sharing Islamic knowledge.

- Ulul-Azm: Refers to the five greatest Prophets: Noah, Abraham, Moses, Jesus, and Muhammad (peace be upon them all).
- Ulama: Islamic scholars who have deep knowledge of Islamic teachings and jurisprudence.

- Usul al-Fiqh: Principles of Islamic jurisprudence used to derive rulings from the Quran and Sunnah.
- Ummah: The global Muslim community united by faith and principles.
- Udhun: Refers to the ear, often mentioned in the context of listening and obedience in Islamic teachings.
- Urdu: A widely spoken language among Muslims, with many Islamic texts and poetry written in it.
- Udhiyyah: The act of animal sacrifice during Eid-ul-Adha in remembrance of Prophet Ibrahim's devotion to Allah.
- Ummi: A term referring to the Prophet Muhammad (peace be upon him) as being unlettered or not formally taught to read and write.
- Uquq al-Walidain: The sin of disobedience or mistreatment towards one's parents.
- Ufuq: The horizon, often mentioned in the Quran in the context of Allah's signs in creation.

V

- Victory (Nasr): Success that comes with Allah's help.
- Virtue: Doing something good and pleasing to Allah.
- Verse (Ayah): A sentence in the Quran that teaches us something important.

- Values: Special rules like being honest, kind, and fair, taught by Islam.
- Vow (Nadhr): A solemn promise made to Allah to perform a specific act of worship or good deed if a wish is fulfilled.
- Volition (Ikhtiyar): The ability to make choices and decisions freely as granted by Allah.
- Validity (Sihhah): The state of an act or worship being correct and acceptable in accordance with Islamic law.
- Verification (Tathabut): The process of confirming or authenticating information before accepting it as true, as taught in Islam.

- Virtuous Deeds (A'mal Salihah): Actions performed sincerely for the sake of Allah, in accordance with His commands.
- Veneration (Tafdhil): Deep respect and honor for something or someone, such as the Prophets or the Quran.
- Visions (Ru'ya): Dreams or sights that may hold spiritual significance, sometimes viewed as guidance or warnings.
- Vindication (Tazkiyah): The act of clearing someone from blame or sin, often linked to personal purification.
- Vigilance (Muraqabah): Awareness and mindfulness of Allah's constant presence and observation.
- Visitor (Zair): Someone who visits sacred sites, such as the Kaaba or the graves of Prophets, with reverence and respect.
- Voluntary Acts (Nawafil): Optional deeds or acts of worship performed beyond the obligatory ones to earn extra rewards.

W

- Wudu: Washing parts of the body to be clean before praying.

- Wisdom (Hikmah): Using knowledge in the best way to make good choices.
- Wa Alaikum Salaam: The reply to "As-salaamu Alaikum," meaning "Peace be upon you too."
- Wahy: Messages from Allah given to prophets through angels like Jibreel (Gabriel).
- Wudu: Washing parts of the body to be clean before praying.
- Wisdom (Hikmah): Using knowledge in the best way to make good choices.
- Wa Alaikum Salaam: The reply to "As-salaamu Alaikum," meaning "Peace be upon you too."
- Wahy: Messages from Allah given to prophets through angels like Jibreel (Gabriel).
- Witr: An odd-numbered prayer offered after the Isha (night) prayer.

- Walima: A marriage banquet or celebration, typically held after the wedding.
- Wajib: Obligatory actions that a Muslim must perform according to Islamic law.
- Wasila: A means of seeking closeness to Allah, especially through prayer or good deeds.
- Worldly Life (Dunya): The material, temporary world in which people live, in contrast to the eternal life in the Hereafter.
- Waqf: A charitable endowment, often in the form of land or property, donated for religious or educational purposes.
- Waqt: Time, often referring to the importance of time in Islam, especially in relation to prayers and good deeds.

X

- Xenophobia: A big word for being afraid of people who are different. Islam teaches us to love and respect everyone!

- X-Ray of the Heart: A way to think about how Allah knows everything in our hearts, even if no one else sees.

Y

- Yaseen: A special chapter in the Quran, often called the heart of the Quran.

- Yawm-ul-Qiyamah: The Day of Judgment when everyone will meet Allah.
- Yusuf (Joseph): A prophet known for his beauty, wisdom, and patience.
- Yaqeen: A strong belief and trust in Allah, no matter what happens.
- Yaseer: A name meaning "easy" or "gentle," sometimes used to refer to the ease of the Quran or life.
- Yaqin: Absolute certainty, a deep and unshakeable belief in the truth of Allah's teachings.
- Yazid: A name that can refer to historical figures, including the controversial caliph Yazid ibn Muawiya.

- Yawm al-Mawt: The Day of Death, the day when every soul will leave the body.
- Yunus (Jonah): A prophet who was swallowed by a big fish and later freed after repenting.
- Yahya (John): The name of a prophet, known for his righteousness and devotion to Allah.
- Yad: Means "hand" in Arabic, often used symbolically for power, strength, or authority.
- Yusuf's Shirt: A symbol of forgiveness, associated with the story of Prophet Yusuf and his reunion with his father Ya'qub.
- Yarmouk: The site of a famous battle in Islamic history between the Byzantine Empire and the Rashidun Caliphate.
- Yamin: Meaning "right" or "right-hand," it can also refer to a pledge or oath in Islamic tradition.
- Yahudi: A term used for Jews, in reference to the followers of the Abrahamic faith.

Z

- Zakat: Giving a part of your money to help people in need.

- Zamzam: A special well in Makkah with blessed water that never runs out.
- Zikr: Remembering Allah by saying His names and praising Him.
- Zuhd: Living simply and focusing on Allah instead of loving too many worldly things.
- Zabur: The holy book revealed to Prophet Dawood (David).
- Zakat al-Fitr: A form of charity given at the end of Ramadan to purify fasting.
- Zamzam Water: Sacred water from the Zamzam well in Makkah, believed to be blessed.
- Zawiya: A Sufi lodge or place for spiritual retreat and worship.
- Zina: Forbidden sexual relations outside of marriage.
- Zindiq: A term historically used for heretics or those accused of holding unorthodox views.

- Zubur: Refers to the Psalms of David (Dawood), one of the holy books in Islam.
- Zaidiyyah: A sect within Shia Islam, particularly in Yemen, that follows the teachings of Zayd ibn Ali.
- Zakat al-Mal: The annual obligatory almsgiving of a portion of wealth to those in need.
- Zikr al-Jami': A comprehensive form of remembering Allah that encompasses both physical and verbal acts.
- Zulfiqar: The famous sword of Imam Ali, known for its unique and distinctive shape.

www.ingramcontent.com/pod-product-compliance
Lightning Source LLC
LaVergne TN
LVHW070049070526
838201LV00040B/411